ANY SKELETONS IN YOUR CLOSET?

A memoir and travelog of a music teacher

MARLA ORR

 iUniverse

ANY SKELETONS IN YOUR CLOSET?
A MEMOIR AND TRAVELOG OF A MUSIC TEACHER

iUniverse books may be ordered through booksellers or by contacting:

iUniverse
1663 Liberty Drive
Bloomington, IN 47403
www.iuniverse.com
844-349-9409

Because of the dynamic nature of the Internet, any web addresses or links contained in this book may have changed since publication and may no longer be valid. The views expressed in this work are solely those of the author and do not necessarily reflect the views of the publisher, and the publisher hereby disclaims any responsibility for them.

Any people depicted in stock imagery provided by Getty Images are models, and such images are being used for illustrative purposes only.
Certain stock imagery © Getty Images.

ISBN: 978-1-6632-1562-8 (sc)
ISBN: 978-1-6632-1563-5 (hc)
ISBN: 978-1-6632-1561-1 (e)

Library of Congress Control Number: 2020925762

Print information available on the last page.

iUniverse rev. date: 12/29/2020

Jack wanted to finish the roll of film in his camera so he said "Go stand over by that little swan so I can take your picture." I walked over, turned toward Jack and smiled so he take my picture but he was laughing his head off.

I said ') ust take the picture." All he could do was point to something somewhere behind me that was out of my vision. I turned yo see what could possibly make him laugh so hard and that's when I saw the danger.

It looked like a 747 was headed right for me. No, it was a 9 foot tall creature with a 7 foot wing span. I couldn't run in my high heels but I tried to back away without falling down.

He statled hitting me with both wings. He was really strong and hitting down hard on my shoulders and arms.

More on that later.

How did I get the idea to write this book? I have always been the genealogist for our family.

When I was about eight years old, my mother received a book in the mail from a cousin who is a Warren. Her cousin had written, "The Warrens and You," which actually had my name in it. I am descended from the Warren, - the Earl of Warren came with William the Conqueror to reclaim England in 1065.

They are listed in 'The Book of Abbey". I was hooked! I read and reread that book and checked the stories. The Earl of Warren's daughter man;ed the son of William the Conqueror and became Queen of England; and two of the Earl's sons married daughters of William the Conquer.

All three lines are traced in history as well as all of their heirs and ancestors.

In addition to tracing all the other ancestors and their stories, I made a "gene" genology. In other words, I traced the cause of death on all ancestors for which a cause was given. I found a first cousin of my mother who died quite young compared to all of the other relatives.

When I asked Mother what he died of she told me "He died suddenly after they all had dinner together." They gave the cause of death as Apoplexy.

In researching this cause I found a lot of cases which could have been anything from a stroke to a heart attack lumped into one large group- "Apoplexy". I determined this was telling me they didn't know the exact cause and couldn't fmd out more.

About this time my Grandmother passed away and another cousin who lived near-by sent me an obit from the Woodward paper which he had laminated especially for me.

I called to thank him personally for the obit and asked if he knew anything about this death I was researching to see if there was a disease running in the family that I had missed or was not aware of. He told me a story I had trouble believing but I know it to be true.

This cousin who died was the Sheriff of Woodward County. I knew that when my mother started to college she lived in town with this cousin, cooked and cleaned for him to pay for her room and board. In fact, she cooked the dinner (lunch) he had the day he died.

I know that my mother could not possibly have put anything in the food that could have caused his death, in fact she was indebted to the cousin for giving her room and board while she was in college.

It seem that years before, he had been called out on a case where a man had been dragged behind a horse until he was dead.

He ruled that it must have been an accidental death. Then later he found out that the two women and the man (now dead) had been permanent!y living together in Dodge City, Kansas. The women were prostitutes and the man was their pimp. One of them must have been very pretty because when she got out jail_the Sheriff married her.

I asked my mother if there could be any truth to that story, to which she declared, "No." That she cooked the dinner herself. And when he got through eating, he went outside to smoke and that's when he just fell down, had a seizure and died.

My mother would never admit that there was anything else to it. My cousin who told me the story insisted my uncle was murdered. Most of the people on the party line think he was murdered. There was never anything else about it in the paper. No autopsies. Make your own conclusion.

I have been told many almost unbelievable stories by other members of my genealogical society because young women will do just about anything to keep from becoming "an old maid" and young men to be able to sign up for the army.

Another of my mother's cousins, a woman, had raised her family and died, and the date of birth engraved on her tombstone was just four months before the date of birth on her sister's tombstone. After I checked the census records I determined one sister had made herself ten years younger and the other sister had "become" twelve years younger.

I found twleve and fourteen year old boys killed in the war after they had "changed their ages" to be allowed to enlist.

Why did I actually start studying Genealogy? That's easy. When our son was born and I was trying to fill out his baby book, there was a page asking for his grandparents' names and their parents' names. I asked Jack's mother if she could tell me her grandparents' names. She told me quite frankly, "No, I couldn't."

It turns out she really couldn't tell me. That enable me to find out how old she really was, and she most definitely not want me to find out her true age. I had already found out she had changed her age on her copy of my husband's birth certificate.

She had been a secretary to the minister of the First Methodist Church in downtown Dallas and had access to white out or whatever secretaries used then. So when I ordered a copy of my husband's birth certificate from Oklahoma City where he was born, I found out she had lied about her age on the original information as well.

I didn't ever tell her because I didn't want to embarrass her, but at that time the census of 1900 had already been released and she was on it AS A 3 YEAR OLD, What a shame for her. Her mother had died when she was six so she didn't think anybody would ever find out how old she really was. She died at 82 without her only child knowing her true age.

But what really got me, when I really got into her family I found that two of her cousins had written genealogy books about their families and both books were in our library. They didn't have dates of births - but they had the children list in order of their bhths.

So it was pretty easy to put 2 years between each child.

I learned in genealogy that young women typically aged only seven or eight years every decade. Nobody wanted to be an old maid. And young boys aged eleven or twelve years every decade. They wanted to join the army and be soldiers.

Jack had four female cousins who lived in Waxahachie Gust a few miles south of Dallas) and he wanted bring me and our four year old son to visit his cousins and show off his new son. They all oohed and aahed over Forrest and said he looked exactly like Jack did at that age.

They all had information to give me about their ancestors for which I will be eternally grateful. But none knew the origin of Dr. Charles L. Orr, Jack's paternal grandfather. He just appeared one day to see after their father.

He was attracted to their older sister and soon asked for her hand in marriage. I have a wedding picture of them. I know everything about her ancestors but not a clue about him before he turned up tn Waxahachie on a doctor call.

I took a wild chance and wrote to the Texas Medical Association and hit gold. A local doctor in Cleburne, Texas, W.M. Yater had mentored him and recommended he goto Louisville, Kentucky to Louisville Medical College (a very large and well known medical school at the time.)

I wrote to that school, giving the mid 1880's as the era, and hit pay dirt. He graduated from medical school in 1886. The Texas Medical Association had made a survey in 1900 of all the doctors in Texas.

I found him in Kenedy, Texas, Karnes Co. southeast of San Antonio, and wrote to the library in Kenedy to see if they had any record of him.

The nice librarian found a picture of him in a scrapbook that some resident had donated, of the seven gentlemen in Kenedy, Texas and a school picture of their two older boys in a class photo. Jack's father was not yet old enough for school. The youngest, Guy, was born in Waxahachie.

All Native Americans had been forced to move (most walked) to Oklahoma Territory from Florida, Georgia and Alabama "The trail of Tears was written about their tragic move.

Oklahoma opened it's doors to nonnative Americans at a slower rate. Joseph Roff had been developing a community in Indian Territory after the turn of the century.

Jack's grandfather thought this was a grand opportunity and transferred his wife and family to Roff which is just outside of Ada, Oklahoma, probably the wealthiest oil town of the early 1900's. All four of their boys played football for O.U. And fought in W.W.I. The eldest became a lawyer, second son managed two hotels in Houston and a radio station in Chicago. Jack's father was a printer in Ada and the fourth son became a reknowned urologist and was chief of staff at a Houston hospital.

During the dust storms and the Great Depression of the 20's and 30's Jack's father and his eldest brother (the attorney) traveled around around all over Oklahoma buying property from folk who were lured to "the land of milk and honey" by land agents back east but who couldn't make a living on the land, and didn't have enough money to go to California.

Bob Kerr Sr. borrowed $500 from Jack's father in the early 1930's to drill his first oil well.

The well did come in and he paid Jack's father back. Then he started Kerr-McGee Oil Company. Later Bob Kerr became Gov. of Oklahoma.

Jack's father died of Lymphatic Sarcoma at Mayo Clinic in Rochester, Minnesota when Jack was only eight years old.

His Mother sold the printing business and moved to Dallas where two of her sisters lived. She put Jack in Dallas Country Day School to board while she went to school. It later merged with St. Marks.

Jack's mother took a room with Mrs. Bywaters (whom she knew from Paris Texas. Mrs. Bywaters' husband had just passed away and her son Jerry was in Europe studying art.

Jerry Bywaters was the longest running curator for the Dallas Museum of Fine Art. He was also on the faculty at S.M.U. On weekends, Jack's mother brought him home with her and he stayed in Jerry's old room.

Jack went to Rice on a full academic scholarship at the age of 16 and graduated from S.M.U. with a Master's in Government. He was a charter member and chapter president of Lambda Delta chapter of Delta Kappa Epsilon (Dekes). We all started having dinner together once a month at nice restaurants in 1994 and continued the dinners until 2019.

Jack served in the Air Force during the Korean War. He was assigned to a joint forces group (Army, Navy, Air Force) guarding nuclear weapons. He had to be armed at all times and could not leave the post.

After the war, Jack took a job with Associated Aviation Underwriters where he worked until retirement.

My mother was born in Amarillo, Texas, but I was born in Woodward, Oklahoma. We moved to Lawton when I was one; my mother still lived in the same house until she was almost 101 at which time she passed away.

This house was about a mile south of the edge of Ft. Sill. When my girl scout troop lost our leader, an officer's wife stepped in as our leader. She took us to interesting places in Ft. Sill that I would never have gotten to see otherwise.

Since W.W.II Lawton has been growing steadily so my class of 1960 was the last year that all of the students were in the same school and the largest class there will ever be at Lawton Hich School.

Since most of the classrooms were very large, we were seated alphabetical order. So I grew up behind Jimmy Lehew. My maiden name is Lehman.

Jimmy is an incredible person and I have so much respect for him. I hope he comes to our class reunion this year which will be our 60th. He was born with a very high I.Q. in a Cherokee tribe, so he was sent to live at the Ft. Sill Indian School.

I have always sought him out at every reunion to see what he is doing and where he is going. At our last reunion he had become a minister.

Two of my grandparents were born and raised in Switzerland; most of my relatives on my father's side have light blue eyes and platinum blonde hair.

The week after high school graduation, my parents took me to the train station in Lawton and I rode the train to St. Louis, Missouri to start college. My piano teacher in Lawton, Dorothy Bell, had enrolled me early in a program at St. Louis Conservatory for outatanding piano students which included private theory lessons, ear training and sight reading every week as well as furnishing all of my printed music from the fourth grade through high school.

During that summer we lived at Washington University and were bused six blocks north in Clayton to the Conservatory. We did all all of our training and testing for four semesters of college music theory, ear training and sight reading so that I aced out of all the music courses for my first two years of college.

Plus, we had lots of recitals by music professors and graduate students. I studied under Leo Siroto who was the artist 1n residence with the St. Louis Symphony.

We got to do a lot of fun things, too. We rode a river boat with a Calliope on it down the Mississippi River and back. We went to a St. Louis Cardinal baseball game.

It was an excellent summer.

Then in September I started at Phillips University in Enid Oklahoma. I got all A's for the work I did in St. Louis. The new piano professor was Jon Nelson who had just gotten back from France studying with Claude Arrieu, who made recordings up into his ninties. He had studied with one of Beethoven's students. That makes me a fourth generation student of Beethoven.

I finished my degree in three years! I played my Senior recital in October and did student teaching on all levels in the spring.

My first room-mate was a girl my age who had been brutally raped when she was 13. Her parents went out to dinner while she babysat her younger sister. My friend was watching her favorite show but her little sister wanted to watch cartoons. (This was back in the cave man days before VCR's.

Her sister made a fuss so she relented and went out to their playhouse out back to watch her program on TV.

Some man watched her parents leave and then followed her out to the playhouse.

She was traumatized when her parents got home and wouldn't let anyone near her.

Her father was a Dr. but she wouldn't let him near her.

I made a mental note not to ever get in a situation like that.

My next room-mate was from India, Sudha Baghowit. She was from a high caste. I never saw her without her sari and a dot on her forehead to prove her status. She wanted to be a Dr. and as soon as she took a few tests she got into a medical school.

When Sudha left I asked if they had anyone who needed a room-mate.

They gave me Monica from Haiti where they speak French. She was lovely and spoke perfect English with a French accent. I loved listening to her talk.

Monica asked if I could give her a perm on very large rollers to straighten her hair. She showed me a perm she had used before. She said everyone does it.

We tried it and she was so happy not to have kinky hair. Tills was in ths 60's. She said everyone in Haiti did it.

I gave my Senior Recital in October for a Music festival month.

After graduation I thought I could get a job teaching in Tulsa. There weren't any music teachers who were going to leave but they said I could make more money as a substitute. They told me to put down everything I felt that I could teach.

Most of my calls were for French or German.

About that time I saw a music store opening on Harvard Ave. in Tulsa: Conn Keyboards. They hired me right away when they heard me play. They wanted me full time to demonstrate and play pianos and organs, teach the free lessons (6 per instrument) and order and stock sheet music and books.

Since neither of the two owners could actually play more than a one-line melody, they really needed me. Plus, (and this is the best thing) they gave me a percentage of all sales since I was in with them from the beginning of the store opening.

I thought I had died and gone to heaven. I got paid for teaching the free lessons and most of the students wanted to keep taking (at my private lesson rate). Some people called in looking for a teacher.

Within a year I had 80 regular students and making more than I could have teaching school.

An Episcopal Church bought our largest church organ. They had four regular pianists who had been playing for the services but none of them had ever played pedals on an organ. I found a time that they could all meet for a group lesson on pedals, got the list of hymns for the next Sunday and made a plan.

Since all of the Episcopal hymns are like Greek to me, and the director takes every hymn at the speed of light, so I had each woman pick one of those hymns to play the pedals on each week. It took a while but I can say that after two months they were getting their confidence up. After Three months their director was pleased with the progress and I don't believe any of the ladies ever dropped out.

One older man, Mr Morton, bought a smaller organ, kept taking lessons, bought a piano, started taking piano lessons as well. He used to play violin on the radio on national radio programs and for commercials. So he wanted to pay me a third amount for accompanying him for thirty minutes on the violin.

I did a lot of accompanying in college but it was expected. I was getting paid for this. Mr. Morton's wife was the head of a cosmetic department in one of the mall stores and she always got me lovely gifts.

But how did I meet Jack?

Jack had always traveled to Tulsa a lot because there are were a lot of corporate jets and a lot of individuals who had their own plane or planes in and around Tulsa. But, I might never have met him if it hadn't been for a fortune teller in New York City.

A fottune teller?

Really!

A man named Jack Galbraith grew up in upstate New York ans his family often rode the train into the "City" to go to the Paramount Theatre to see a movie but mainly to watch the organ rise up out of the orchestra pit between movies or extras with Don Baker sitting at the organ and playing fabulous music.

The organ Don Baker was playing there was the Long Island University WurliTzer, a 4 manual, 26 ranker shipped on June 20, 1928.

WurliTzer produced only 2 organs of this size, the other instrument still resides in the Boston Music Hall.

Although used almost until the closing of the theatre, the organ had deteriorated considerably.

The Brooklyn Paramount opened on November 23, 1928, it was the Capstone of architects Rapp and Rapp. It's sheer opulence outdid anything preceding it with : Lattice eilings and arches in gold, festooned with artificial foliage, concealing the Wilfred Color Organ (that changed lighting color and intensity with music); chorus girls ascending and descending to the stage on golden staircases in front of the organ grills on either side; an elaborate proscenium curtain below a majestic grande drape, done in blue velvet with polychrome satin pheasants; stage and orchestra elevators, and a dual console mighty WurliTzer on separate lifts.

It was when it opened, second largest theatre in New York City.

In 1969, the New York Chapter of the American Theatre Organ Society reached formal agreement with Long Island University to restore the organ. Led by member Bob Walker and his crew, it sang forth in all it's original glory for the American Theatre Organ Society Fabulous Fifteenth Convention in 1970.

Since then, it has been used for several concerts, recording, and TV programs as well as all Long Island University home basketball games. The console remains on it's lift and comes up through a trap door in the floor of the basketball court.

You can see why Jack Galbraith and his family wanted to come to New York City to hear Don Baker. And they probably had a favorite place to eat before catching the train back to their home town.

And somewhere along the way they always came to a fortune teller who always told Jack Galbraith he was going to die when he was 76.

When Jack Galbraith had his 75th birthday he happened to remember what that fortune teller had told him years ago. When he opened the newspaper that morning his eye caught a picture of Don Baker who had started working for Conn Organ Co. (electronic) and who was playing a concert at our store on a theatre style organ that we were selling.

I took some lessons from Don Baker both in Tulsa and later in Dallas when he played at the Kochise Music Store on Preston Road at Forest where I worked later on.

At Conn Keyboards our first customer when that model came out, was a Mrs. Blanton, whose husband had recently passed away leaving her tons of money.

She used to play for silent movies at a theatre in Oklahoma City. After hearing Don Baker play the one in our store, she ordered one in Antique White and Gold.

I was on point to go to her beautiful home and show her how to use the special effects and rhythm section.

She could play circles around me, as could Don Baker, but I knew how to get her using the gadgets and changing the stops.

Mrs. Blanton was so appreciative that she wanted to give me her music cabinet from her days at the theatre in Oklahoma City. It had 50 shelves two inches apart, filled with "lead sheets" and various other music. I didn't have any place to put the cabinet, she had been keeping it in her garage, but I saved almost all of everything else that was in it.

There were some lead sheets (one piece of paper that came to the theatre with each silent movie telling the musician what was going to happen and two or three measures ofthe kind of music to play).

And I saved all of the frrst editions of popular sheet music from that age. Someday, I will probably sell some of the things to collectors and get rich.

Then the next time I went to he home, she had some designer clothes to give me. Her husband had set her up with a shop to sell designer clothes. She got tired of it but kept all of the clothes. I was really well dressed for a while.

There was a church we thought might buy a theatre organ model. It was what I thought of as a Holy Roller church. They wanted a demo so we took the model to the church for a Wednesday evening service at 6:30.

A musician was already playing a grande piano really well, so I sat on the bench of our theatre organ, someone told me the page number and I joined in on the theatre organ. I put on the Leslie speaker (a revolving speaker built into the theatre model) and made it sound like I knew what they wanted.

I had never heard any of the hymns they sang and we played, but as they changed to different songs I figured out the key and played right along like Ihad known it all my life.

After about an hour of this some of the people started rolling around on the floor (I had heard of Holy Roller Churches _ now I had participated !) Everyone acted like they loved the organ.

They kept singing and speaking in tongues. About 10:00 Mr. Wheeler (the non musician owner) told me I could go on home, that he would load the organ up and take it back to the store.

I hope they bought an organ. I certainly did my part well. It's a lot of money for a small church - but if they really want it, they can fmd some way to buy it.

Jack Galbraith had moved to Tulsa years before; he and his wife had opened an insurance agency at the Tulsa

International Airport and handled all of the insurance and reinsurance for everyone at the airport.

Jack's had turned 56 and remembered what the fortune teller had said. He didn't really think a fortune teller could tell how long he was going to live; but when he saw Don Baker's photo in the paper he was interested in hearing him again.

His wife had never heard Don Baker play the organ so she was enthusiastic.

Jack Galbraith came to our concert and loved the idea of learning to play the organ.

He did buy a small spinet organ and started taking lessons from me.

Jack Galbraith started taking the lessons. He was a fast learner and his wife, Marge, always came with him to listen and to encourage him,

A few months later Marge started talking about a guy they knew who would be perfect for me. I had been "fixed up" for a blind date with two different guys that were real duds, so I always had excuses ready.

Mr. Galbraith had traded up twice to larger instruments and he was still taking lessons.

I came out of my studio late one night after I had finished teaching, and went up to my desk at the front of the store to get my purse. There was a note on my phone to call Mrs. Galbraith.

It was 8:30, I was tired, but I called Mrs. Galbraith and had my excuse all ready, "I'm sorry I didn't get your message in time" she said "we're just leaving - see you in five minutes." And she hung up.

I thought "What just happened? Do I have another blind date?""

I brushed my teeth and combed my hair, and unlocked the front door of the store because my students usually got dropped off at the front. I sat down at my desk. And when Jack walked in I couldn't believe it. He looked like a possibility!!!!!!!!!!!

I had so much fun and later after we were married, he said he wanted to marry me as soon as he found out I went to church every Sunday. I said that when you're the organist or pianist you don't get to decide each week if you are going to church.

When I told him they had just poured the foundation for my house, he said "Let's get some food and have a picnic on your slab!"

It was quite a while before I could finish my house enough so that I could sell it. Jack, in the mean, time wrote to me every single day and came to Tulsa as often as he could. I thought he must be serious. I KNOW that he was is serious about me.

I designed several of the light fixtures and hung wallpaper in several rooms. I rented an organ and a piano to teach on while I was finishing my house.

Jack Galbraith DID have a heart attack when he was 57, but it was a mild one and he got to the hospital quickly.

When Jack gave me an engagement ring, the president of the company, Bob Yeargin, flew down to Dallas in the company jet to take us out to eat at The Cattlemens Steakhouse to celebrate.

Mr. Yeargin told me not to get too comfortable in Dallas because we "would probably be moving to New York in three to five years."

That was A-OK with me. I could picture living in Manhattan in a smallish apartment and going to Broadway shows every week.

We built a new house that would be likely to sell fast because we both owned homes that were unusually difficult to sell. I didn't even put up pictures on the walls for years.

Jack worked on his golf game and we joined Prestonwood Country Club. I loved listening to Jack tell stories about his clients-- really rich plane owners that you wouldn't expect to be so funny.

Well the Koch brothers weren't really, really funny but they were really, really nice. Jack was in Tulsa briefly to check something with the Galbraiths and was headed to Koch Industries the next morning but Tulsa was weathered in.

He called Koch to see if he could post-pone their appointment that morning until the next week. Charles Koch said, "don't worry. I'll just send the Lear down to pick you up."

Jack was so impressed. Nobody had ever come to pick him up for an appointment. And the pilot even let Jack fly from the right seat! He had flown the Lear in a simulater but not in real life.

Jack knew personally virtually everybody in the five-state area who owned a plane. That's a whole lot of people.

He let it slip earlier that he wouldn't insure women pilots or doctors. Women in general, couldn't keep their emotions under control in an emergency; and doctors thought they could handle anything, so they didn't check out the plane thoroughly before taking off.

Well, he didn't put it quite that bluntly, but he had to do a lot of soul-searching before he would insure a woman.

Then, he started working on his instrument rating, flying in all kinds of bad weather. His instructor was married to a woman pilot who taught instrument training with him. In fact, they both went with us to the first Superbowl that the Cowboys played in!

It was in Miami and he could write it off as part of his instrument training for a long distance flight. I felt really safe with three pilots (two of whom were instructors) on board. She was an excellent pilot as well, so that put an end to his not insuring women pilots.

Jack was the manager of the five state region of Associated Aviation Underwriters and the largest region outside of the home office, which was in New York City, a block away from where the twin towers were to be built.

We stayed in hotels in that area many times. And we had friends whose children had jobs in buildings near-by who told us about the trauma they had to endure to survive. I am certainly glad we never had to move to New York.

Jack Orr underwrote all of the insurance for all of the planes that Jack and Marge Galbraith in Tulsa insured. They were the only insurance agency based in the Tulsa International Airport, so they got all of the business at the airport.

Jack Orr underwrote for several other insurance agents in Tulsa. So he was there frequently.

Jack and Marge Galbraith gave us a big brass elephant for a wedding present. I still have it sitting where it has always been - on a side table in the foyer.

As I said earlier, Jack Galbraith DID have a mild heart attack when he was 57. He later had cancer and then eventually died after having a stroke. Marge lived about ten years after he passed away. We kept in touch and took her out to eat every time we were in Tulsa.

In 1987 the Nuclear Power Plant at Chemobyl had a near melt-down. It put out so much waste a huge cloud formed which was deemed ubsafe to fly through. All airlines had to change their routes.

We were on a 747 coming back from Europe that had to change routes twice because the cloud was moving.

We eventually had to land in Reykjavik, Iceland and refuel before we could continue to Dallas. Iceland was beautiful and a magical place to visit. We enjoyed our time ther however short.

The most fun I ever had dancing was in Heidelberg, Germany in the basement of a large build where tour groups joined up for good German food and music.

The dancers were really good. The men all had on their traditional Leiderhozen (seude short pants with fancy suspenders). At the end of one song the dancers split up and picked new partners from the audience to dance with.

The man who was the best dancer grabbed my hand and started doing the polka with me. That was absolutely the most fun I have ever had dancing

As soon as I caught my breath I spoke to him in German.

Two of my grandparents were born and raised in Switzerland so I took two years of German to be able to read our German Family Bible. Was est Autsgeseichtnette!

The second Super Bowl the Cowboys played in was in New Orleans before the Super Dome was built. It was played in the football stadium at Tulane University.

It was a last minute thing for us to get to go. A friend in New York had gotten tickets, and then something came up and they couldn't go. He literally gave us the tickets. But there were absolutely no hotel rooms available.

One of the agent in New Orleans that Jack had always reinsured had grown up in New Orleans, and they still owned the old family home in the lake district. His mother was in a retirement home at that time so they offered to let us stay in their old home for the week-end. There was a Poinsettia tree in front of the house that had grown all the way up to the second floor roof.

It was a gorgeous home with wonderful old furniture including a feather bed with a canopy top in the master bedroom. All of their elegant crystal, china and silver was there. We weren't planning to eat there and I didn't dare touch anything.

Our friend was a member of a crew for Mardi Gras and had collected memorabilia from many Mardi Gras in the past and photos were displayed everywhere.

There was a marriage certificate for his ancestor on the wall, dated 1728!

The stadium was only about six blocks away and we could ride the trolley to the game. After the game it was a mad house of traffic, so we just walked back to the house.

The next Superbowl the Cowboys were in at New Orleans was at the new Super-Dome but on a weekend with turbulent weather. Coming into Lake Front Airport we had a little trouble - well, we had a LOT of trouble.

We were flying over Lake Ponchartrain pretty low to stay under the turbulence and all of a sudden we would lose altitude and be headed straight for the lake. Jack would grab the controls and get straightened out and before I knew it we were headed down again.

Back up. Level out. Check the ailerons. On the straight and narrow.

Here we go down again. And then corrected back up. Hardly any rough water, not even any little waves.

Now we are going almost straight down. Jack grabs the controls and gets us buildings at the airport because of the rain. Here we go again. Down and then up.

I don't think we're going to make it. Jack's got it. He has set the autopilot so he could look at the map/book to fmd the setting for the radio to contact ground control, but the ailerons in the autopilot keep turning themselves off.

Here we go again! Straight down! Now Jack is getting us straightened out. He'd better not ask me to drive. I don't think I can do this. I could see the airport but I've never landed over the lake like this. could see the runway - - - I knew it was built out over the water.

I think I can swim to the shore. There we go again, straight down. Jack's got it. Back up.

I take off my shoes, can't swim in those. And I get my drivers' license out of my purse and put it in a pocket on my blouse. Oops. Down again. Jack pulls us back up.

Here we go down again.

Back up. Straightened out. Jack is contacting the airport.

Good! They can come out to get us if we go down.

And the ailerons went off again. Here we go down.

About 15 minute more of this and we landed XXX:X or I mean Jack got us to dry land!!! We were at the airport and I didn't even have to swim. But it was touch and go.

And we beat the Denver Broncos the next day!!!!!!!!

The Denver Broncos fans were all upbeat and so glad to have made it to the Superbowl. Even though they lost, they were happy! And that made it more fun for everyone!

As opposed to the year before. The Steelers' fans had gathered in the motel bar the afternoon before the game, and when they found out we were from Dallas - they wanted to fight!

They were all men! I was not! That didn't matter to them! They actually tried to get Jack to go outside and fight!

Jack somehow smoothed out the situation. But the next day at the game - at half-time, we became aware from other Steelers' fans that some of the travel agents from Pittsburgh and the suburbs had either double booked or outright cheated their Steelers' fans.

All of those fans had to find some other place with a TV to watch the game! We made a quick and accurate decision not to go back to the room after the game. We had a lovely dinner at Joe's Stone Crabs.

Sam Walton was a typical businessman who resided in Benton, Arkansas. Well, he wasn't really typical; he was much smarter than most.

You can tell from the way his business expanded so rapidly that he was really, really good at it.

He knew how to treat his employees and his store managers. He liked to visit them often, probably unplanned and unannounced but not secretive. He wanted to see how things were really going.

Sam flew his own plane and he frequently took his bird dogs with him in case the store manager wanted to hunt birds with him.

On the way back to Benton, Sam noticed that something was wrong with his plane. He went to find his manager, who took care of his plane.

"Hank, thurz sum pin wrong with ma plane. I ain't got no raydeo. Nuttin works. Ken ya get it fixt up?"

"sure thing Mista Sam, I'll get it fixt rat up."

For those who are not pilots, the radio is all of the non-physical operation of all controls; in other words, he had no way to talk to air-traffic controllers, or to check altitude, direction, or even how much gas he had.

Two weeks later.

"Didja git it fixt?"

"Thur workin on it rat now Mista Sam. Hadda take it on over ta Memphis ta git the rat parts."

"Did they know whut happen to it?"

"no Mista Sam, they ai n't seen anathing Iak it before."

THREE MONTHS later.

"Mista Sam? I think they got yer plane fixt." "Sure tuckim a long tam. Did they say whut was wrong in the furs place?"

"Mista Sam, they say it lookt lak sumpin had chew up all a the wirin'."

Long pause!!!!!!!

Sam got a funny look on his face and finally said, ' Well, twern't MA DOGS!"

And it turns out, it wasn't Sam's dogs that did it.

When they had put the store manager's dogs in the plane, there wasn't room in the back luggage compartment with his own dogs in it.

They had to put the store manager's dogs in the front luggage compartment which also contained all of the wiring for the whole plane! And his manager's dogs had never flown in a plane before so they were nervous.

After Sam got his plane back and was gone on another trip, Jack was at the airport for other business, when the manager asked Jack if he had ever seen Sam's car that he left at the airport when he was off flying on other business.

Jack said "No, I can't say that I ever have."

He took Jack to where Sam always parked his car while he was off in his plane.

It wasn't an old car, it had just been used a lot, or rather, it had been abused a lot.

The seats all had stuffing pulled out through rips, the doors and dash board were scratched beyond repair, the head liner was hanging down all around the edges.

The window control inside the car was hanging by the wires. It still worked – it was just hanging loose by the wires.

When we finally got the opportunity to ride in a 747, we went to Scotland to play golf with about ten other couples.

We loved the experience of playing on the courses so beloved by the Scottish and English golfers.

After we had finished playing the last course, we rode the high-speed train to Gatwick Manor.

We spent the night there, ready for the return trip to Dallas.

Our luggage was already being loaded onto ow· 747, and after a leisurely breakfast, we went outside by a beautiful little pond where Jack wanted to finish the roll of film in his camera.

Jack said to me "Go stand over by that little swan so I can take your picture." I gingerly picked my way across the thick turf in my high heels.

As soon as I got near the little swan I turned toward Jack to smile for the camera.

But he was not focusing his camera. He was laughing his head off. I said, "go ahead and take the picture."

He was laughing so hard, I could see tears in his eyes. All he could do was point to something out of my vision and more back behind me.

I turned toward what he seemed to be pointing at and immediately started backing away from what appeared to be the largest animal I had ever seen, with a long neck stretched up straight, wings spread out wide and running on the tippy toes of his huge flipper feet.

I never want to face anything like that again as long as I live. This was not an ordinary swan. This was a daddy swan who had been protecting his babies from being kidnapped, for way too many years. In fact, he was probably one of the "Seven Swans a' Swimming from the Twelve Days of Christmas."

We were in New York City for a quarterly meeting of the branch managers and wives. The meetings were over but we had extended our stay so that we could see some shows and museums (and maybe I could shop.)

It was quite warm outside and we decided to stop in a bar to get a cool drink. There weren't any seats at tables but there were two empty bar stools at the long bar.

We headed for the bar stools and Jack picked the empty stool to the left by the blonde woman. I headed toward the stool on the right beside a well-dressed black man.

I soon struck up a conversation with the nice man who asked what we were in New York for?

I told him and somewhere in the conversation I told him I was a piano teacher.

He said "I play the piano a little."

Something just told me there was more to the story. I turned slightly and looked him right in the face and said "Oh my gosh!

You are Erroll Garner!!! I have all your records and I love to hear you play!!!!" I reached out to shake his hand.

I couldn't believe my luck at not only sitting by him, but at conversing with him and recognizing him as well. He's not the kind of person to go up to a stranger and tell them he is a famous pianist.

Erroll Garner is assured a place on anyone's short line of important and influential pianists. If one considers an original and lyrical style, an infectious sense of rhythm (with a knack for swinging), and an extraordinary improvisational prowess as appropriate standards of true jazz genius, then they are very ably met by Garner's life and art.

For Gamer, there was always music that needed to come out. From his early beginnings as a child prodigy in Pittsburgh, Pennsylvania (born June 15, 1923) where attempts at traditional music training were foiled by his remarkable ear and an incredible aural memory_his new and original style would develop and become a dominant influence on contemporary piano.

At age seven, Erroll began appearing regularly over Pittsburgh radio station KDKA, and by the time he was eleven, he was substituting for riverboat pianists on the Allegheny.

In his early teens he began a succession of jobs in and around Pittsburgh in taverns, nightclubs and restaurants, usually performing solo.

Marla Orr

By the early '40s Erroll had moved to New York, winning attention in the thriving nightclub scene there.

On March 27, 1950, Garner became one of the first jazz instrumentalists to give a full evening's recital in a concert hall, performing solo at The Music Hall in Cleveland to critical raves and a standing ovation.

Subsequently, he appeared as guest soloist with numerous orchestras throughout the United States, and his programs of improvisations became highlights of the international concert circuit.

Most notably, Garner was the first and only artist from the jazz idiom to tour under the aegis of classical impressario Sol Hurok, who directed Garner's concert appearances from 1955 to 1962.

His career as a concert performer, headliner and composer would, very simply, flourish continually in the United States for almost four decades.

French critics called Garner "The Man with Forty Fingers," while other Euoropeans referred to him as "Chaplinesque" and "The Picasso of the Piano" in tribute to his wry musical excursions and unique, personal style.

Of the more than 200 compositions Garner wrote, some of his best-known tunes are: "Misty", "Dreamy", "Solitaire", "Feeling is Believing".

His premature death on January 2, 1977, at the age of 53, left a legacy of inspired live performances, numerous recordings, and enduring memories of his spontaneity, imagination, and joy.

=

Consider the praise of Duke Ellington, who, in assessing Garner's lyrical voice, declared, "He was not only a pioneer but an innovator with an identifiable sound".

Nobody will replace him or erase the distinctive mark he has made on American music.

I am so glad I sat by him and had the wonderful memory of meeting him.

I have so many memories of places I have been, people I have met, and stories I have read.

And I have the memory of going down into a bunker built into a cliff that Hitler had built for the purpose of spying on the English and U.S. Troops during World War II.

And I've also touched a portion of "the Wall" that Hitler built to divide East and West Berlin. So many people died because of that wall.

When we were at the Tulsa International Airport having lunch with Jack and Marge Galbraith, someone recognized Jack and told him that Pan American (whom Jack's company insured, had just taken posession of the very first 747 and were testing it out.

They wanted to see how it would react landing on an icy runway.

Tulsa had an icy runway they didn't need that day so they told Pan Am to bring it down. It landed fine until they tried tried to turn. Then the left tire slid off the runway, and sank about ten feet down in the mud.

They asked if we would like to come out and see it. They pulled a jeep around and took us out to the plane. It was so-o-o-o big! About half of the wheel was down below the top of the runway!

The wheel was big enough for a full size automobile to drive through the middle. They had the exhaust corning out under the wheel so it was plenty warm for us.

One of the big questions was "how were they going to get the plane up out of the mud? Jack had a very good idea.

There were so many oil companies based around Tulsa, and they always had cranes big enough to lift a drill out of the ground. So they contacted somebody who deals with the cranes.

While we were waiting for one to get there, they asked us if we would like to look at the inside of the 747. Yes, we certainly would.

We climbed a ladder up through the middle of the radio (all of the wiring for the whole plane) and came up into the cockpit.

In movies now days you get to see things like that, but it was so new and huge that it took our breath away.

We went into the body of the plane and felt like we were in an auditoreum!

Not very many civilians got to have this experience. I felt so lucky to have met Jack at this time in history.

The crane arrived and lifted the plane just like it was a little toy!

While we were planning the new campus our church built, Rev. Oliphint gave a wonderful sermon on faith, even as a grain of mustard seed.

The ushers passed out packets of mustard seeds for us to take home with us.

It was such a great sermon and just what we needed to hear. The only problem I had was that the choir was singing from the balcony in the old building and the ushers didn't make it upstairs to give the choir members some mustard seeds.

As we left the sanctuary I went out the front entrance to ask the ushers if I could have some mustard seeds to give to the choir.

They gave me some which I took back to the choir room, giving them out to to choir members I passed in the hall.

By the time I had taken off my choir robe and put my music away, the next service had started and I couldn't get back out the way I had planned.

I had to go a longer way around the sanctuary to get to where Jack had parked the car.

In the street I spotted something that looked like a fancy toy ring, probably costume jewelry, but I picked it up, and called the church office as soon as I got home.

I wanted them to announce that someone had found a ring but she said "no. Lost and found doesn't belong in the church service but if someone asks me if anyone found a ring, I will give them your number."

I stayed close to the phone all afternoon and most of the next day, but nobody called.

The next day I needed to pick-up my watch from the jeweler's so I took the ring with me to see if it was worth putting an ad in the paper.

Anyone could have been crossing the street there, it could have been someone going to church, or a jogger, or someone going to the shopping center across the street.

The jeweler said he couldn't tell - it was so dirty, so he cleaned it and looked at it with his loop and said, "Yes, these are real diamonds and quite a few. It looks like an anniversary ring and it's probably worth around $6,500."

Wow, so I put it in a safe place and called the church again to see if anyone had responded. It was a different person so I gave her all the information again.

I started writing an ad to put in the church paper, and one for the Dallas Morning News but I was going to give it a few days.

On Thursday, a member of our church called and said hls wife had lost two rings. I asked hlm to describe them and the ring I found was definitely one of her rings!

He was there in five minutes and we were both so happy! She was elated and sent me many gifts and even theatre tickets. It really gave me a good feeling to fmally fmd the owner.

The Sunday she lost it, she had fixed breakfast, fed the baby, gotten all of her children bathed and dressed for Sunday School, her husband couldn't find a parking place. So, he dropped them off at the door and said he would meet her at the usual place in the Sanctuary.

It was twenty or thirty minutes before she realized that her rings were not on her fmgers.

Her husband kept telling her that she had her mustard seeds! Now she just had to believe that her rings would be found.

I kept telling myself that I had the mustard seeds so I would be able to get the ring back to her. I love a happy ending!

When I was in the fourth grade, I found out I could write to the Tourist Dept. at any state capital and ask if I could get some information on interesting places to visit for a vacation in their state.

So we planned a trip together with them through New England, and then Philadelphia. That fit in with my fifth grade cuniculum.

Then, we visited Mother's middle brother who was a petroleum engineer living in Denver. He knew all the really nice spots in Colorado.

I accidently, laid my sunglasses down on top of Pike's Peak where we were getting hot chocolate in the snow in August. I have never found another pair of sunglasses I liked as well as those, but it taught me a life lesson about keeping my possessions organized and in place.

Next was through the desert at night to California. My mother lived in California for a short time when she was young. But we saw a lot more of it than her family had.

My mother was great at organizing our trips and making sure we saw all of the things we wanted to see.

Next time we went to see Aunt Elouise she planned a trip to Washington D.C. I felt so lucky being able to tell all my friends about all the wonderful places.

I've sung mass at St. Peters, St. Marks, St. Francis of Assisi, two cathedrals in Switzerland, the National Cathedral in Washington D.C., the Abbey church at Fontevrault where exist the effigies of Richard the Lion-Hearted, and his queen, Berengaria, Henry II and his queen, Eleanor of Aquitaine.

I have visited Notre Dame Cathedral in Paris three times but they don't allow choirs to sing there.

I have seen the Sahara Desert, and the Great Salt Plains.

I've visited in: all of the states in the United States before I turned 16; Jack and I visited Alaska and Hawai which weren't states yet when I set up my first goals in the fourth grade.

I have visited in all of the State Parks, sailed across all five of the Great Lakes, swum in the Great Salt Lake, played all of the great Golf Courses in Scotland, Spain, and California, sailed up the west coast of Africa, sailed across the Atlantic Ocean, Pacific Ocean, Baltic Sea, and Caribbean Sea.

I have visited in Aruba, Australia, Barbados, The British Isles, England, El Salvador, Estonia, Denmark, France, Holland, Hungary, Iceland, Italy, Jamaica, Norway, Sweden, Russia, the Canary Islands, Cape Verde, Madeira, Ireland, Morocco,

Gibralter, Malaga, Granada, Portugal, New Zealand, StThomas, Scotland, Sicily, and all the Hawaian Islands.

I have visit all of the palaces in Russia, Great Britain, Sotland and France.

We rode under-water in a submarine to view the Great Barrier Reef.

We flew down to Mexico many, many times because it is close to Texas: Acapulco, Baja California, Guadalajara, Los Mochis, Manzanillo, Mazatlan, Puerto Vallarta, Tijuana, Veracruz, Mexico City.

The Texas Insurance Convention was held in Mexico City in 1972. They chartered a whole plane so they could take all those who wanted to go.

We visited in Australia, where I got to snuggle with a cuddly Koala, and feed baby Kangaroos.

I've lived for more than six weeks in Angelfire, New Mexico, Camp Crowder, Missouri, St. Louis, Missouri, Woodward, Oklahoma Dallas and Richardson Texas and several places in Oklahoma when I was too young to know.

In Monaco, Jack wouldn't let me gamble even though I felt lucky.

In Paris we visited the Notre Dame Cathedral as a choir, but we were not allowed to sing in it. There is so much to see and history we needed to hear that we were awed anyway.

I've visited in these major cities:

Antwerp Belg. Barcelona, Sp; Belfast, N.Ire;

East and West Berlin, Ger;

Berne, Switzerland, Bordeaux, France Budapest, Hungary; Casablanca, Morocco, Dresden E.Ger. Dublin, Ireland;

Essen & Frankfort, Ger

Genoa, It. Glasgow, Scot.

The Hague, Netherlands

Hamberg, Ger. Helsinki, Fin. Leeds, Eng. Leipzig, E. Ger Leningrad, Lille, France

Lisbon, Portugal Liverpool, & London Eng Madrid, Sp.

Manchester, Eng

Marseille, Fr. Melbourne, Austrail ia Milan, It.

Monterrey, Mex.

Montreal, Can. Munich, Ger. Naples, It Newcastle, Eng. Ottawa Can., Palermo, It Paris, Fr.

Perth, Australia

Potl-Au-Prince, Haiti, Quebec City, Can. Rome, It.

Rotterdam, Neth.

San Juan, Puerto Rico Sevilla, Spain, Stockholm, Swed. Stuttgart, Ger

Sydney, Austrailia

Tijuana, Mex. Toronto, Can. Toulouse, France Turin, It. Valencia, Sp. Vancouver, Can. Vatican City, It.

Venice, It 3 times

Vienna, Austria 3 times

Winnipeg, Can.

Zurich, Switzerland 3 times.

We went under Niagra Falls in a boat from Canada (U. S. boats don't go under the Falls).

We used to eat out every night and one of out favorite restaurants was L'Ancestral in Highland Park. We almost always saw somebody there that we recognized.

This particular evening was a Saturday and there were only two empty tables, both on the left side which was all mirrors.

It was nice because you could see everyone in the whole restaurant.

Jack dropped me off at the door while he parked, and they seated me at the second table and I was facing the door so I could see Jack when he came in.

Just before Jack got there a beautiful woman came in and was seated at the first table facing me. I was trying to think of her name - it was on the tip of my tongue. I could see her picture up on a wall someplace I visited regularly.

I finally got it. Her picture was in the foyer of the building my OB Gyn had moved into, at Presbyterian Walnut Hill. It was Margot Perot! The had paid for the new building.

Jack came in just then followed by Ross Perot. Ross had his offices on the top floor of the large glass building at Park Central so that he could use the heli-port on top of the building. Jack had the floor right below his.

And when he got to us he said "You insured all my aircraft Jack Orr and had your offices right below mine."

Every time I see him I think of Dana Carvey imitating Ross on Saturday Night Live when he was running for President. And Ross said to Dana "you do me better than I do."

When SouthWest Airlines was just starting up, they came to Jack to under-write their insurance. Jack spent about three days going over everything thoroughly, then sent it to the president of the company for approval.

The President of the company called Jack immediately and said "H------ No-- I'm not going to insure an airline that only has three planes."

Jack had to call SouthWest back and apologize. They had to go to someone else to get insurance that year.

A year later, they had five planes and they called Jack back. He got the approval this time.

But the best thing for Jack's office was his thorough check of the pilots, etc.

The president of the company who turned Jack down that first year, he himself insured an eastern start-up company which only had TWO planes. And the first year they lost BOTH of them!

We had better pilots at SouthWest Airlines. And I don't think SouthWest has ever lost a plane. Kudos to SouthWest!!!!

SouthWest invited us to a lot of big celebratory dinners but the first one was a really big shendig dinner to celebrate the successful finish of their first year.

There were several hundred people at this event - everybody who had anything to do with SouthWest.

The surprise entertainer was BOB HOPE! It seems he was born the year airplanes were invented. He was so funny and since this event was not televised he didn't have a filter on his language; he was even X- rated. I won the door prize for our table, a model of their first 737.

The first time wives were invited to a managers' meeting at Associated Aviation Underwriters was the spring of 1971.

Gen. Sweetser, The Angeles Manager of Jack's company was retiring and A.A.U. took this opportunity to invite all of the managers' wives to attend with their husbands in L.A.

The Executive Vice President of A.A.U. Will Daly, volunteered his new wife, Gloria Swanson Daly, to be in charge of charge of entertaining the wives the first evening.

Gloria looked just like her mother, the movie star of old, except that she was much taller and was really very sweet.

Jack was sure Gloria would take all all eight women to "her" restaurant, The Brown Derby, which she had inherited from her father.

Gloria thought it would be far too complicated to have us transported that far across town and back for that many ladies.

Instead, she took us to Trader Vic's because it was just across the street from our hotel. Most of us had a Trader Vic's in our own city so it was nothing special.

Jack took me to the Brown Derby later because he wanted to see it.

But at the next manager's meeting that the wives were included, she made up for it. This one was held at Marco Island Florida.

Gloria had stayed here with her mother many times so she was greeted by most of the residents as she was escorting us to shopping and places of interest.

Then in Palm Springs she took me shopping at 'Alan Ladd's Hardware Store'. I bought a tiny crystal pitcher (it would hold syrup for one pancake, I still have it.)

Then in 1989, Will had retired and they bought a house on the golf course at Cypress Point. We were their guests to play golf there and at Pebble Beach.

One of the other entertainments A.A.U. arranged for the wives in Palm Springs California was a tea with Elliot Roosevelt, the youngest son of Pres.and Mrs. Eleanor Roosevelt. Elliot has written a whole series of mysteries in the White House with his mother as the heroine.

Elliot made specific provision in his will that none of the books can be released as long as any of the people the characters are based on are still living.

When Jack found out I used to play at a restaurant, he asked me to play something for him. I said "What is your favorite song?"

When he said 'As Time Goes By", from the movie "Casablanca."

I asked him, "How does it go?"

I thought Jack was going to come unraveled!

I thought I was going to come unraveled.

I was almost 30 years old, had a degree in music, worked at a music store, stocking sheet music, played in a restaurant.

But I had never heard of Jack's favorite song.

It turns out, I wasn't lying.

I hadn't ever heard Jack's favorite song because it had been banned in Oklahoma. In fact I found out all movies with Ingrid Bergman, had been banned as well as all books by John Steinbeck!

Oklahoma didn't like the fact that Ingrid Bergman had given birth to a child fathered by her director, while her husband was back in the states. Also, they didn't like the way Oklahoma was portrayed in "The Grapes of Wrath"! So they banned all of John Steinbeck's books and movies and all of Ingrid Bergman's movies.

I grew up in a sheltered environment and didn't even know it until I met Jack.

What an education. I made up for it by memorizing Jack's favorite song and watching the banned movies I had missed, on late night T.V. IN TEXAS.

I feel betrayed! I thought I had a very good education.

All of the bragging I had done about my education was tainted.

Where did our educational system get so far off the track.

What else did I miss out on?

When somethlng like that hits you, you begin to question everything.

I guess I have always questioned everything.

That's why I am such a voracious reader.

Printed in the United States
By Bookmasters